A Jot Journal for the Forgetful, Easily Distracted, Disorganized, and/or Discouraged

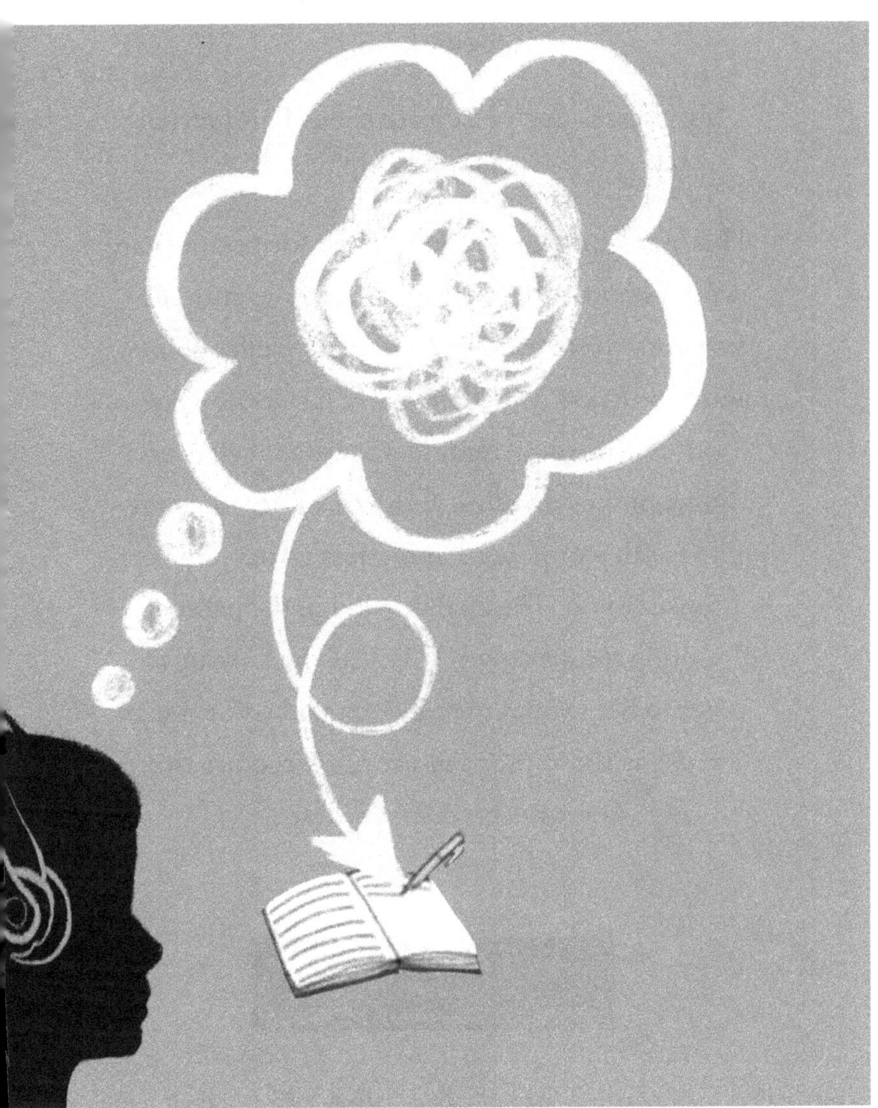

Like the cover says, this journal is for the forgetful, easily distracted, disorganized, and/or discouraged.

My guess is you're a creative too. This journal should help.

This blank and lineless jot book is for people who work best under their *own* unique structure. It's very easy to write down reminders, bullet points, and a to-do list. Whether you're just jotting down words, little note reminders scattered all over, bullet points, doodles, sketches, or neat squares filled with words, all that matters is that it makes sense to you. The goal is to get in the habit of writing things down. Follow up by looking at notes to help you remember great ideas or things to do, without the pressure of a structure that works for someone else.

©

## Paris Loves Books

Do you have an idea for a personalized journal? We can make it a reality:

www.parislovesbooks.com
@paris.loves.books on all platforms

www.ingramcontent.com/pod-product-compliance
Lightning Source LLC
Chambersburg PA
CBHW070628081025
33728CB00027B/704/J